MADELINE ISLAND ABC BOOK

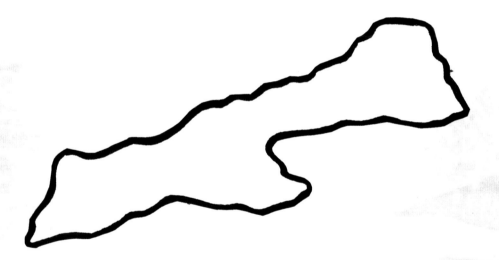

WRITTEN BY
MARCIA HENRY

ILLUSTRATED BY
SALLY PARSONS

This project is supported by a grant from the La Pointe Center, which has received its funding from people of this community, The Wisconsin Arts Board and the State of Wisconsin.

SALP

First Printing, First Edition

Library of Congress Control Number: 2007902106

ISBN: 978-1-4243-3753-8

Printed in the United States of America by:
Service Printers of Duluth, Inc.
Duluth, MN

Published in the United States of America by:

LOON
COMMONS
PRESS
P.O. Box 182
La Pointe, WI
54850

Dedication

From Marcia: This book is dedicated to my seven grandchildren whose visits make summers worth waiting for - Lauren and Matt, Kris and Sarah, Lexe and Maeryn, and to Cole (who has yet to visit this remarkable place) - and to their Grampa Burke, the love of my life.

From Sally: In memory of my grandmother Effie Taylor, my mother, Effie Parsons, my uncle, Frank Taylor, and my still very much alive aunt, Virginia Schmidt, this book is lovingly dedicated. They all were part of a magical childhood spent on Madeline Island.

Acknowledgements

We gratefully acknowledge the La Pointe Center and the Wisconsin Arts Board for their encouragement and support of this project. Thanks to Steve Cotherman and Sheree Peterson at the Madeline Island Historical Museum and to the Madeline Island Historical Preservation Association for sharing interesting historical information with us.

From Marcia: Thanks to Marj Ellison Smith, proofreader extraordinaire and "oldest" Island pal, who again volunteered her expertise. It was Marj and her parents, Vera and Pokey Ellison, who first made Madeline Island memorable for me some seven decades ago! And, I consider myself extremely fortunate in working with Sally Parsons who made the ABC book come alive with her exceptional illustrations.

From Sally: I'd like to thank my family and friends for the constancy of their encouragement and belief in creative efforts coming to fruition, however late the bloom. A special thanks to my sister April and her husband Todd and my sister Sue for providing me safe haven in which to work and enough light with which to see. Also, a very special thanks to Marcia Henry whose inspiration this book has been. Her unflagging encouragement and upbeat enthusiasm has helped bring a lifelong dream to reality.

Note: The watercolor still life inset on the second page of "V" was done by Effie Parsons in the summer of 1989 while vacationing on the Island and remains a favorite of her daughter. It is fitting that her work be included in this book.

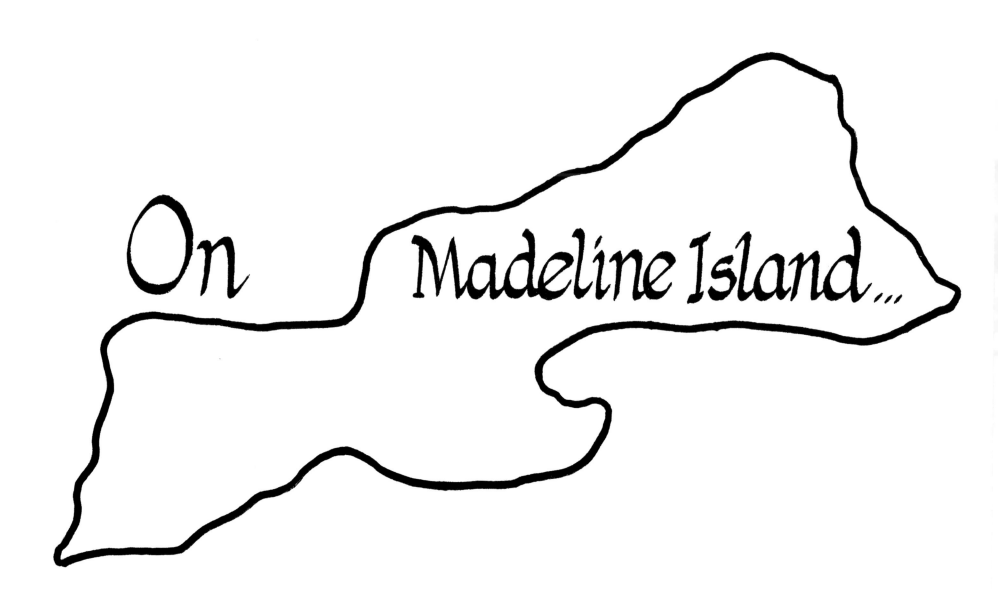

On Madeline Island...

Aa

Artwork and Artists can often be found. In Autumn the Apples and Acorns abound.

Bb

There are Butterflies, Bears,
Beavers and Bark,
Boats, Bikes and Birch trees
and Big Bay State Park.

For C there are Cabins and Camping,
Cardinals and Canoes,
Chickadees, Cherries
and even Cuckoos!

Cc

CRANBERRY BOG RENTALS

Dd

D is for Dugout,
Docks, Ducks and Deer
Daffodils and Dogsleds
with Doggies so dear.

Ee

Equaysayway was named
Madeline, it is said,
as Eagles and Egrets
soar high overhead.

Gg

Geraniums and Gentian
in Gardens Galore;
with Geese on the Golf course
you'd better yell "fore!"

Hh

History and Heritage,
Horses and Hammocks;
there are Herons and Hummingbirds
and even some Hemlocks.

I is for Island, both Princess and Queen,
with winter's Ice Angel
they make quite a team.

Madeline Island Ice Angel

Ice caves, Ice fishing,
Ice roads: they're all seen.
Just wait until summer...
there's even Ice cream!

Jj

Enjoy Junipers and Jasmine
near Julian Bay,
Joni's Beach and Jazz concerts,
also Juncos and Jays.

JONI'S BEACH

Kk

*Kayaks with Kayakers
skim by on the lake.
Kingfishers and Kites flying high
while beach bathers bake.*

Ll

There's a Lighthouse and Lilacs,
La Pointe and the Loons.
You can dance in the moonlight
near Big Bay Lagoon.

Mm

Visit Museum and Marina
and Madeline's summer Music camp.
Watch Mallard and Mink frolic
near the Manitou fishing ramp.

Nn

There are Nesting Nuthatches:
red-breasted and white,
Nature and New moons
and Northern Light Nights.

Oo

Ojibwe once settled
these fresh water shores,
Finding Oaks, Owls and Otters,
they passed down their lores.

Pp

*Pedal or Paddle
among the green Pine,
then Pitch your Pup tent
and all is divine.*

Qq

Quince Jelly
1 Quart

Quilting Bees

Mondays & Thursdays 10 to 4

"Honey"

Quilting QueeriBee

Queen bees and Quilts,
rock Quartz and Quartets;
the island rock Quarries—
have you seen them yet?

My brother told me to quit quibbling about each little ache and pain and go see Doctor Quinch. But from what I hear, he's a bit quaint. What do you think?

Well I question his practices. I personally think Doctor Quinch is a "quack." He doesn't seem to know his quinine from his quinacrine hydrochloride.

...and then they began quoting recipes for quiche and quickbread until I thought they'd give us all a quiz...it was all so funny...

Oh Perceval! You keep me in "stitches" with your hilarious stories!

Hmm...I've got questions about how to play quoits, what to do in a quake, and how to build a Quonset hut. And I'm having qualms about how to quash a quarrel with my sister Qu'en. Seems like I'm on a personal quest.

Quenton, quilting is not quick. You'll hear quips, queries, and, sometimes, even some quarrels. But it gives you a chance to observe people...their quirks and queer behavior...we are all a bit odd. That's okay. Don't quit now. The quality of our quilting is what is important, and that is quintessential. You won't find better.

Rr

Recycle an old Rowboat.
Ride a Red Rocking horse.
Where do you find them?
On the island, of course.

There are Raccoons near Red Cliff,
a Rose garden display.
Pick Raspberries, watch Robins
on a hot summer day.

Ss

Summer Sun invites Sailboats
and fun in the Sand,
winter Snow: Sledders and Skiers
criss-crossing the land.

Tt

There are **T**urtles that bask
in the sun at **T**own Park.
We play **T**ennis, watch **T**ugboats
'til **T**wilight's last spark.

Uu

Stay Under your Umbrellas
if you visit in the spring.
See Uncle Sam ride a Unicycle
in the July 4th fling.

V v

Vacationing Visitors have a Veritable feast where once Voyagers' canoes paddled furs north and east.

Xx

The eXtensive collection of eXceptional books at the eXcellent library — It's worth eXtra looks.

Yy

You'll see Yachts and Yawls
with Youngsters on board,
Yellow warblers and Yarrow
near the York Island shore.

Zodiac and Zephyr
(that soft island breeze),
Zucchini and Zinnia,
they all start with Zs.

A Brief History of Madeline Island

Since the last glaciers retreated from the area 10,000 years ago, many groups of people have lived in the Apostle Islands region of Lake Superior. Beginning in about 1490, the Ojibwe settled here, regarding Madeline Island as their sacred home. Ojibwe is the English name for these Native Americans. Other names are Ojibwa, Ojibway, Anishinaabe and Chippewa. In early times, they depended upon the abundant natural resources of the lake and woodlands for food, clothing, tools and shelter. They canoed and traveled about the islands and mainland, setting up seasonal camps for fishing, hunting, and berry picking and sugaring the maple trees. They built birch bark lodges on Madeline Island where they gardened, processed food and animal skins, and spent the long winters. The Island was also a gathering, trading and meeting place for Ojibwe relations and other tribes.

Beginning in about 1690, a great cultural encounter occurred when first the French, and later the British and Americans, moved into the area and made contact with native inhabitants. The great fur trade era began as these new groups of people traded mass-produced and machine-made goods such as sewing needles, mirrors, multicolored glass beads, and guns for the pelts of fur-bearing animals supplied by the Ojibwe. Pierre Le Sueur founded a trading post on the south end of Madeline Island near where Grant's Point exists today. The settlement of La Pointe became an important trading center. Cultures blended as marriages took place between fur traders and Ojibwe people. Michel Cadotte was a famous French-Canadian fur trader who married an Ojibwe woman named Equaysayway in the early 1800s. Her father, Chief White Crane, decreed that the Island be named Madeline, Equaysayway's Christian name.

Catholic and Protestant missionaries came to the Island in the early 1830s. Following them were American and European immigrants, many from Scandinavia, who came to settle in the area. They built homes and started industries such as brownstone quarrying, commercial fishing, boat building and logging. Many of the Ojibwe families left in the mid-1850s under the terms of the treaty of 1854. By the 1890s, people began to discover the Apostle Islands as a vacation destination. They built summer cottages on Madeline Island, such as the beautiful homes on *Nebraska Row*.

The first schools on Madeline Island were mission schools supported by Protestant and Catholic missionaries in the 1830s. Public schooling on the Island probably started around 1860. A new school, the Bay View School, was built around 1873. Thirty-three children attended the school in 1880. Beginning in 1913 children traveled to school in a horse-drawn wagon and in winter in a horse-drawn canvas-covered sleigh. Bay View School closed in 1927 and was moved several blocks from its first location. It now houses the Island Library.

In 1899, the Christensen School opened near what is known as Russell Bay. It closed in 1908, reopened in 1926, and then shut its doors for good in 1938. The third public school built on the Island, Lakeview School, opened in 1904. It was located on one acre of land at the corner of where Big Bay Road and Schoolhouse Road now exist. Lakeview also closed in 1938. After that all children attended the new Bay View School in the village of La Pointe. Lakeview School was donated by its owner to the Madeline Island Historical Preservation Association (MIHPA) and is now part of MIHPA's Heritage Center. Children now attend the La Pointe School in grades K-5. The "new" Bay View School makes up the center portion of the present school. Older children attend the Bayfield Middle School and Bayfield High School.

Today Madeline Island has a year-round community as well as thousands of seasonal visitors who travel back and forth to the Island by regular ferry boat service. Ferries run by the Madeline Island Ferry Line also carry the middle school and high school students to Bayfield. When, and if, Lake Superior between La Pointe and Bayfield freezes more than eight inches, the ferries stop. Then the windsleds take over as the lake freezes and again as it thaws. In between, residents and visitors to the Island drive their cars on the ice road. A van transports the students and others who do not drive on the ice road.

Madeline Island remains a special cultural site for the Ojibwe who celebrate their ancestral traditions on the island. The rich history and natural beauty of the Island make it a very special place for all who live and visit here. We hope you enjoy your visit to Madeline Island either in person or through this book.

Information courtesy Madeline Island Historical Museum-Wisconsin Historical Society and the Madeline Island Historical Preservation Association.

An excellent resource for more information on Madeline Island, first written in 1960 and now reprinted, is *La Pointe: Village Outpost on Madeline Island* by Hamilton Nelson Ross.

An Alphabet Treasure Hunt for Island Detectives

You will be looking for alphabet treasures all around the Island. Be sure to respect private property. The local and state parks have their own rules about where you can hike. Most parks ask you to refrain from changing or removing any natural material such as sticks, nests, feathers, rocks or plants. Please follow these rules carefully.

Also, keep the Island clean.
Leave any candy wrappers, lunch bags, cans or other litter in the trash bins located throughout the Island.

We hope you enjoy your Madeline Island treasure hunt and
the *Madeline Island ABC Book*!

Directions: Look for the treasures below as you visit Madeline Island, or look for some of the objects in the pictures in the book.

You can also learn a little bit about the sounds that letters make. Most letters in the alphabet are called *consonants*. The letters a, e, i, o, and u are the primary *vowel* letters. Vowel letters have both a "short" sound (marked in a dictionary with the breve symbol ˘) and a "long" sound (marked in a dictionary with a macron ˉ).

A, a – A is adorable! A can say /ă/ as in *apple* and /ā/ as in *acorn*. See if you can find Island items beginning with the letter **a** such as *accordion, acorns, acrobat, actor, actress, afghan, airplane, airport, alder, altar, amaryllis, ambulance, anchor, angler, animals, ants, antenna, antler, anvil* (Hint: Look at the Heritage Center), *aphid,* another *Apostle Island, apple trees, apples, aquaplane, art and artists (visit the Madeline Island School of Art (MISA) and the La Pointe Center/Art Guild Gallery), aster* and *aurora.*

List other words beginning with "**a**" that you find: _____ _____ _____ _____

B, b – B is beautiful! Can you find Island items beginning with **b** such as *baby, backpack, badger, badminton, bald eagle, balloon, balsam fir, band* (check out the 4ᵗʰ of July parade), *bank, barge, bark* (on a tree), *barn, baskets, Basswood Island, bay, bats, the Bayfield (a ferry boat), Bayfield (the town), beach, beach glass, Bear Island, beaver, beaver dam, bees, beetle, begonia, bell, bench, berm* (look for the *berm* near the airport), *berries, berths* (see the *boats* in their *berths* at the Marina), *bicycles, Big Bay Town Park, Big Bay State Park, bikeway, birch, black bears, blossoms, bluebirds, blue jays, boardwalk* (walk the boardwalk at Big Bay State Park), *boats, boathouse, bog, bratwurst, breakwater* (look in the harbor where the ferry boats dock), *bridge, brown creepers, brownstone, buck* (the male deer*), bugs, bullfrog, bumblebee, bumper* (on a boat), *bunkbeds, buoys,* and *butterflies?*

List other words beginning with **b** that you find: _____ _____ _____ _____ _____

C, c – C is captivating! C has two distinct sounds, /k/ and /s/. Look for **c** words with the /k/ sound: *cabins* or *cottages, cabin cruisers, calla lilies, camel* (Yes! There is a *camel* on the Island), *camera, Canada geese, canoe, canopy, canvas, captain* (look for the ferry boat *captains*), *cardinal, carnation, castles* (visit the State Park's day for making sand *castles*, or build one of your own), *catamaran, caterpillar, cattails, clarinet, classroom* (visit the LaPointe Elementary School or the old one-room Lakeview School at the Madeline Island Heritage Center sponsored by Madeline Island Historical Preservation Association [MIHPA]), *clinic, coastline, comet, compass, conifer* (any evergreen *cone*-bearing tree), *constellation, cormorants, County Trunk H, cranberries, cranes, crayfish, creel, creepers, crib, crickets, crows, cuckoos,* and *cumulus clouds*.

Can you find words beginning with **c** where the **c** has the /s/ sound? Watch for *cedar, cemetery* (drive out Middle Road to Greenwood *Cemetery*), *ceramics, cicada,* and *cirrus* clouds. (NOTE: c usually has the /s/ sound when it comes before an e, i, or y.)

When c is followed by h, it can say 3 different things. The main sound is /ch/ as in *church*. Here are some words beginning with **ch**. How many can you find on Madeline Island? *chamber music, Chamber of Commerce, charter, cheese, cherries, chestnuts, chickadees, chimneys,* and *churches*.

Ch can also say /sh/ as in *chef* when it comes from the French language. (Check out the *chefs* at local restaurants.) You might also meet someone from *Chicago*.

If **ch** is in a Greek based word, it says /k/ as in *chorus* and *choir*.

List other words beginning with **c** or **ch** that you find: _____ _____ _____ _____

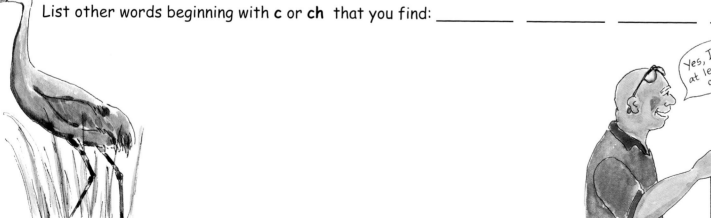

D, d – D is dandy! Can you find the following items beginning with **d**? *daffodils, daisies, dandelions, dawn, deck, deer, deer mice, displays* (Visit the Madeline Island Historical Museum), *divers, docks, dogs, doe* (a female deer), *dragonflies* (also called *darning needles*), *driftwood, drydock, ducklings* and *ducks* and *dump trucks.*

List other words beginning with **d** that you find: _____ _____ _____ _____ _____

E, e – E is elegant! E can say /ĕ/as in *elephant* and /ē/ as in *event*. Find these items beginning with **e**. *eagle, eaglet, earthworms, eaves, egret, eiders, elderberries* (Find berries near the boardwalk at Big Bay State Park), *emu*, the *Exchange* (find treasures to keep), and *evergreens*. There may even be an *eclipse* of the moon or the sun.

Did you find any other items beginning with **e**? _____ _____ _____ _____ _____

F, f – F is for Fun! Look for the following items beginning with **f**: *fairway* (find the lovely Madeline Island Golf Course), *falling stars, farm, fawns, feathers, fern, ferryboats, fins, fir trees, firecrackers on the Fourth of July, fireplaces, fish, fish nets, fishhooks, fishermen, flags, flickers, flowers, flies, fog, foghorn, foresail, forest ranger, fox, Franklin stove, frogs,* and *full moon.*

What else can you find that begins with **f**? _____ _____ _____ _____ _____

G, g – G is gorgeous! G, like c, has two sounds. G can "say" /g/ as in *go*, or /j/ as in *ginger*. The g usually has the /j/ sound when it comes before the letters e, i, and y.

See how many items you can find that begin with **g** having the /g/ sound: *gable* (Look at some of the old homes on Nebraska Row), *galaxy* (the Milky Way is right overhead), *gallery, gardens, garter snakes, gazebo, Gazette, geese, gifts* (gift shops abound, just look around*), golden rod, goldfinch, golf course, grackles, Grant's Point, gravel pit, great horned owls, great grey owls, grebes, grocery stores, grouse, guitars* and *gulls*.

Now look for **g** words where the **g** has the sound of /j/: *gentian (bottle and fringed), geocache* (go to www.geocaching.com to find the Island *geocaches*), *geraniums,* and *gypsy moths*.

In a few words the **g** is silent. Look for *gnomes*, and get rid of pesky *gnats*.

Can you find other items whose names begin with **g**? _____ _____ _____

H, h – H is hilarious! Find *hammocks, harbor, harriers, hawks, hemlock (trees & flowers), Heritage Center, heron, herring gulls, hibachi, hornets, horse flies, horses, hulls, hummingbirds, hunters, Huskies,* and *hydroplanes*.

List some other items beginning with **h**: _____ _____ _____ _____ _____

I, i – I is illuminating. I can say /ĭ/ as in Indian, and /ī/ as in *ivy*. See if you can find the following: *Ice Angel, ice cream, ice road, icicles, impatiens, Indian grave yard, insects, Island Queen,* and *ivy*.

Are there other Island objects beginning with **i**? _____ _____ _____ _____ _____

J, j – J is a joker. Look for *jam* or *jelly*, *jibs*, *jonquils*, *juggler*, *juncos* and *Joni's Beach*.

What else can you find beginning with **j**? _____ _____ _____ _____ _____

K, k – K is kicky. You'll find *kayaks*, *keels*, *kestrels*, *kiln* (visit Woods Hall), *killdeer*, *kindling*, *kingfisher*, and *kites*.

Did you find other things beginning with **k**? _____ _____ _____ _____ _____

L, l – L is lucky. Can you find *La Pointe*, *ladybugs*, *lagoon*, *lake*, *landing strip* (drive by the airport on Big Bay Road), *larva*, *leaves*, *leeches*, *library*, *licorice*, *library*, *life jacket*, *life preservers*, *lifeboat*, *lighthouse*, *lilacs* and *lilies*, *lily pad*, *limestone*, *lizards*, *log cabins*, *logs*, *loom* (visit Woods Hall Craft Shop and watch the weavers), *loons*, *lupine*, and *lures*?

Look for other interesting words beginning with **l**. _____ _____ _____ _____

M, m – M is marvelous! Search for the *Madeline (a ferry boat)*, *Madeline Island Historical Museum*, *mainsails*, *mallards*, *maple trees*, *marigolds*, *marina*, *mast*, *mayflies*, *meadow*, *mergansers*, *meteors*, *mice*, *mink*, *monarch butterflies*, *moon*, *mosquitoes* (we hope you won't find too many!), *moss*, *moths*, *mopeds* and *motorcycles*, *mud*, *mushrooms*, and *musicians* at the *Music Camp*,

Find more things that begin with **m** on the **m** page. _____ _____ _____ _____

N, n – N is nifty. Watch for *nature trails*, *Nebraska Row*, *nests*, *nets*, *Nichevo*, *night hawks*, *North Star (Polaris)*, *northern lights*, *northern pike*, *Norway pine*, and *nuthatches*.

What else can you find that begins with **n**? _____ _____ _____ _____ _____

O,o – O is oodles of fun! O can say /ŏ/ as in *otter* and /ō/ as in *oboe*. Observe *oak trees, oars, Old Glory (the American flag), orchards, ore boats, osprey, otter, outboard motors, outhouse, ovenbird, owlets* and *owls*.

Are there other objects you see beginning with **o**? _____ _____ _____ _____

P, p – P is pitching in and looking for *paddles, pancakes, pansies, parade, parks, pebbles, peonies, pergola, petunias, pileated woodpecker, pine cones, pine needles, pine squirrels, pine trees, police officer, police car, pond, poplar trees, poppies, porches, portholes, Post Office, potbelly stove, potter's wheel, pottery,* and *pup tents*.

When p is followed by h it has the sound of /f/. You might find *pheasant, philodendra, phoebe* and *phlox*.

What else did you find that starts with **p**? _____ _____ _____ _____ _____

Q,q – Q is quizzical! Notice that q is almost always followed by the letter u. Look for *quarries, quartets* and *quintets, quartz, queen bees* and *Island Queen, quilts* and *quilters, quince,* and *quivers*. Also, read all of Sally's *quotes* on the **q** page!

Did you find anything else beginning with **q**? _____ _____ _____ _____ _____

R,r – R rocks and rolls! Watch for *raccoons, rafts, ragweed, rainbows, rainstorms, raspberries, raven, Recreation Center, red-tailed hawks, restaurants, rhubarb, robins, rocks, roses,* and *rowboats*.

Record other things you find starting with **r**: _____ _____ _____ _____ _____

S, s – S is scintillating! See if you can seek *sailboats, sand, sandhill cranes, sandpipers, sandstone, salmon, schools, schooner, scooters, seaplanes, skipping stones, skis, snakes, snapdragons, snipe, snow buntings, sparrows, spiders, spinnakers, stars, spruce, sunflowers, Sunset Bay, swan, swim suits* and *swimmers.*

And in winter: *skates, skis, skiers, sleds, snow, snowballs, snowmen, snowmobiles, snowplows* and *snowshoes.*

The s followed by an h has a different sound /sh/. Look for *ships, shooting stars,* and *shore.*

You'll find lots of other things beginning with **s**, including: _____ _____ _____ _____

T,t – T is terrific! Take time to find *tadpoles, telescopes, tennis courts, tent caterpillars, tents, tepees, terns, toads, Town Hall, trails, tripods, trout, tulips, tugboats* and *turtles.*

T followed by h has two special sounds /th/ as in *thistle, thicket,* and *thrush* or /<u>th</u>/ as in *this, them,* and *those.*

Write what else you find beginning with **t**: _____ _____ _____ _____ _____

U, u – U is unique! U can say /ŭ/ as in *umbrella* and /ū/ as in *unicycle.* You can look for *ukeleles, umbrellas, umpires* (watch a ball game at the Rec Center), and *Uncle Sam* and *unicycles* as you enjoy the 4th of July parade.

On the **u** page you'll find these plus people *upside down, undercover, underwater,* and in *underwear!*

See if you find other unusual objects starting with **u**: _____ _____ _____ _____

V, v – V stands for vitality! Be on the lookout for *visitors* on *vacation*, *vegetable gardens*, *vines*, *violets*, *violas* and *violins* (plenty of these during the Music Camp weeks) and *Voyageurs* (watch the *video* at the Museum).

What else begins with **v**? _____ _____ _____ _____ _____

W, w – W is wonderful! You may see *water*, *waders*, *warblers*, *wasps*, *waves*, *waxwings*, *weasels*, *weather vanes*, *weavers*, *winches*, *windmill*, *woodpeckers*, *wolves* and *wrens*.

When w is followed by h it has the sound of /hw/ as in *whispering*, *whitefish*, *white pine* and *white-tailed deer*.

Search for other **w** words: _____ _____ _____ _____ _____

X, x – X is eXcellent, but few words begin with x. Maybe you can draw a *xylophone* in the sand. Look at the **x** page for book titles containing **x**.

Can you think of other works beginning with or containing **x**? _____ _____ _____ _____

Y, y – Y is yummy! Look for *yachts* and *yawls* (visit the Madeline Island *Yacht* Club), yarrow, yellow birch, yellow jackets, yellow warblers, yew, yoyos and *YOU*.

List some other words beginning with **y**: _____ _____ _____ _____ _____

Z, z – Z is a zig-zag and razzle-dazzle! You won't find *zebra* in a *zoo*, but you may find *zinnia*, *zithers*, *zoom lens*, and *zucchini* and the *zip code* 54850.

Do you know other words containing **z**? _____ _____ _____ _____ _____